ANCHOR BOOKS

ALL THINGS BRIGHT & BEAUTIFUL

Edited by

Rachael Radford

First published in Great Britain in 2003 by
ANCHOR BOOKS
Remus House,
Coltsfoot Drive,
Peterborough, PE2 9JX
Telephone (01733) 898102

All Rights Reserved

Copyright Contributors 2002

HB ISBN 1 84418 082 4
SB ISBN 1 84418 083 2

FOREWORD

Anchor Books is a small press, established in 1992, with the aim of promoting readable poetry to as wide an audience as possible.

We hope to establish an outlet for writers of poetry who may have struggled to see their work in print.

The poems presented here have been selected from many entries, and as always editing proved to be a difficult task.

I trust this selection will delight and please the authors and all those who enjoy reading poetry.

Rachael Radford
Editor

CONTENTS

The Song Of The Brook	Joyce Dawn Willis	1
Rookery	Paul McGranaghan	2
The Garden Mole	Rosalind I Caygill	3
The Devious Donkey	Celia G Thomas	4
Zoo Time	Hugh Campbell	6
That 'Cooking Fat'!	Martin Buckley	7
Thoughts For The Season - Summer	M D Bedford	8
Summer	K Forcey	9
Little Dog Lost	Irene Beattie	10
Pussy Cat	V J Haynes	11
A Resident's Tail	Barbara Dunning	12
The Horse	Olivia Kim Ruth King-Cook	14
My Dog Lucky	Rachel Gallagher	15
A Dolphin's Life For Me	Mandy Craven	16
The Kingfisher	Steven Krzymowski	17
I Am A Cat	Joan E Blissett	18
Barney - A Tribute	Pat Gooding	19
Paunce's Poem	Jo Brookes	20
Our Pet	Caroline Halliday	21
Summer Is A-Coming In	Alma Montgomery Frank	22
The Seasons	K Taylor	23
Green Hills	Edith Buckeridge	24
Bright Autumn's Pantry	Hazel Mills	25
Summer Holidays	Patricia McBride	26
Our Holiday	P R Baker	27
Summer	Gareth Thorpe	28
Summer Holidays	Linda Evans	29
Hide And Go Seek	Roy A Millar	30
Summertime	R Burden	31
Crispin	P Clinton	32
Cats In Snow	Margaret Ballard	33
Our Four Legged Friends	Lesley J Worrall	34
The Great Blue Fish	L Howarth-Kirke	35
Rigsby Fat Cat	Evelyn Balmain	36
Animal Thoughts	Derek B Hewertson	37

Sam	Mary Parker	38
My Love Of The Sea	Deborah Coltman	39
The Salmon	K K Work	40
Thoughts Of A Squirrel	Roger Williams	41
Cats	E M Eagle	42
Whitey	Neil Mason	43
Lady - My Old Dog	Linda Ann Marriott	44
Oliver Kitten	Susan Lewis	45
A Puppy's Tale	Julie Hampson	46
The Stare	Jeannette Kelly	47
My Dog	D Kirk	48
My Cats	Ann May Wallace	49
Sandy Mac'Tavish	Elwynne	50
Flowers	Dorothy Margaret Smith	51
The Eagle And His Mate	Irene Hartley	52
Night Sky	Zoiyar	54
Nature	Jean P McGovern	55
Summer Evening Magic	Gwyneth Pritchard	56
My Dog Jax	Anne Davey	57
Houdini	John Green	58
The Elephant	Molly Phasey	59
Two Pets	Angus Richmond	60
The Shade	Derek Budd	61
Digging	Walter Dalton	62
Norfolk Pigs	Geoffrey S Wilyman	63
My Dog	S J Dodwell	64
Sunny	B Smith	65
A Dog's Prayer	Dot Ridings	66
The Sheltie	Peter P Gear	68
Reflections	Lynda Burton	69
Cats	D Adams	70
Secret Love	Maureen Arnold	71
The Joys Of Getting Old	Brian Lorkin	72
Puppy Love	A J Witherington	73
The Butterfly	Toni Attew	74
Gardening	Thelma Jean Cossham Everett	75
Despondent Autumn	A Gwynn	76
Seeds Of Life	Pam Samways	77

Title	Author	Page
Foot And Mouth, 2001	Winsome Mary Payter	78
The Tree	Kathleen Rose Ferguson	79
Our 'Burmese' Dilemma	Susan Carline	80
Buster	Patricia Biggs	81
Gnasher's Revenge	D J Jasper	82
Cats	Kathy Rawstron	84
The Island Of Samos	Jennifer H Fox	85
The River	Doreen Moscrop	86
Walk With Me	Rachel Lowery	87
Greedy Cat	Gail McClory	88
My Tortoise Snoopy	Joan Edwards	89
Ode To My Dog	Eileen E Whittaker	90
'Sooty' - A Beloved Cat	Avril T Hogg	91
Cats And Kittens	Anna Parkhurst	92
Herbie	Amanda Richards	93
The Pheasant	R T Owen	94
My Cat	Gladys Mary Gayler	95
Walking The Dog	Gary Pike	96
Garden Birds	Pauline M Parlour	98
The Missing Ravens	Loré Föst	99
Define A Canine	Dennis Overton	100
Moon	Trevor Howarth	101
My Hamster Kevin	Carly Rosewell	102
The Garden	Joyce M Robinson	104
Gus	Nicolette A Bodilly	105
Beauty	Kathleen Cork	106
Sunflower	Sue Pearce	107
Transience	Christine Lemon	108
Changing Scenes	Joan Wright	109
A Sting In The Tail	Helen Walker	110
Strolling	Eddie Lawrence	111
An Evening Walk	Pat Hayward	112
The Rose	Catherine Watson	113
Mother Nature	Mark Wood	114
I Spider	Maureen Gilbert	115
A Dewdrop On A Rose	M Newble	116
A Pony Tale	Jean Ledwards	117
How Can I Work?	Angela White	118

A Dog's Life - Through Petra's Eyes	Ann Nelson	119
Skylark	D W Mynott	120
Taff My Friend	B Green	121
Cats	Gemma Doughty	122
The Yearly Clipping In June Of Seymour Butts . . .	Lesley S Robinson	123

THE SONG OF THE BROOK

In winter its song is never heard,
under ice it sleeps with never a word.
Covered with a blanket of white snow,
awaiting for the cold winter to go.
And when the warmth of spring begins,
ice cracks and the little brook sings.
Lapping and splashing, gurgling away,
sun glittering on its silvery spray.

Near its embankment small birds sing,
colourful butterflies flutter on wing,
serenaded by the brook's rippling song,
happily it gurgles and trickles along.
Lapping and splashing it gently weaves,
between wildflowers and windswept trees.
Moonlight reflecting on the brook below,
after darkness has melted sunset's glow.

When the golden sun gilds the morning sky,
Millstreams brook still ripples close by.
Sparkling like diamonds by the sun's ray
forget-me-nots and ramsons lining the way.
God blessed us with such beauty and flare,
the fragrance of flowers growing with care.
Birds praising songs, brooks rippling near,
to mix with the peace and tranquillity here.

Joyce Dawn Willis

Rookery

Black webs scored on a sky of steel
Knotted nests in naked trees
A burnt out, growling bird-filled creel
Ravens calling down the breeze

Knotted nests in naked trees
Woven from the mouths of birds
Ravens calling down the breeze
A dark cocoon of raven words

Woven from the mouths of birds
Calligraphy of branch and bough
A dark cocoon of raven words
Air is the soil that ravens plough

Calligraphy of branch and bough
A burnt out, growling bird-filled creel
Air is the soil that ravens plough
Black webs scored on a sky of steel.

Paul McGranaghan

THE GARDEN MOLE

The animal I write about
I've actually never seen
When walking down the garden path
It's obvious he's been.

When down the lawn I pass
Blooms are strewn upon the grass,
To see the flowers lying around
The results of your work under ground.

Next morning when I make my rounds
The little earth thrower's numerous mounds
Have sprouted up just everywhere,
It's really more than I can bear.

Beetles, slugs, earthworms beware
This little fellow can easily scare
You with his soft brown fur
Nose sniffing in the air
Fur combed and sleek
Pattering on his tiny feet.

My feline friends, the cats next door
Sense the activity beneath the floor,
Heads turning this way and that
Following the creature's winding track.

Sadly we'll have to set some traps
To catch these naughty little chaps.
I only hope dear Mr Mole
That you, will make another hole
Perhaps in some farmer's field
So your fate may not be sealed.

Rosalind I Caygill

The Devious Donkey

The frank expression in his eye
Belied the fact that he was sly,
Rather like a Jekyll and Hyde,
Rarely showing his darker side.

When Mother nursed him at her knee,
She coached him in duplicity -
How to look sad and cry on cue
Whenever there was work to do.

After learning his ABC,
He read up on chicanery.
Researching devious schemes became
His first concern, his private game.

He masterminded clever tricks
To use when he was in a fix,
Faking his falls on rocky roads
To tip out all the heavy loads.

The high sierras were too grim
And definitely not for him!
Mountain climbing would never be
His favourite activity.

On market days he wore a look
Of innocence as he partook
Of carrots - pilfered every time -
A misdemeanour, not a crime.

While other donkeys strained their backs,
He thought it safer to relax
Under a jacaranda tree,
Lulled to sleep by a buzzing bee.

As he slumbered, he dreamt that work
Was obsolete - no need to shirk!
Time to throw his panniers away
And make siesta last all day.

Celia G Thomas

ZOO TIME

It was started by humans and animals too,
For ended, by going, one day to the zoo,
The time took, so long, did go,
Through the night,
When the first deer of Heaven
Gave of their delight,
The cold streams on high, were impeccable,
Astounded the natives who all came, to blame,
The lions and tigers, who fought in their name,
My mum, was an emu, the best to be had,
I know little, or nothing about my said dad,
He came, and he went, all through the night,
And told, of his prowess, with all, of his might,
Might it be, but night, it seems,
Whenever an ostrich goes there, through your dreams,
Chased by, on high, of the elephant man,
Who'll do all the catching, as best that, he can,
Then the feeding time begins,
Lots of cold and yellow tins,
You've got to eat, or be of hunger,
When I was three, I was no younger,
Or was it four, who keeps the score,
I've seen all the cages and bars, that I need,
And if in December, or was it November,
They're to heighten our perches,
For those who can stand,
I've sometimes forgotten, that once I was free,
But now, with my wings clipped
Close to the bone,
I'm here in my cage, bird age of, alone.

Hugh Campbell

THAT 'COOKING FAT'!

Does what he likes; when he likes.
Has food, love and attention.
Lives inside the house, like me.
But in an 'Else' dimension.

If I've a cold; then it's alright.
You know what men are like.
They always moan. Leave them alone.
In fact; 'Go take a hike!'

But if poor 'pussy' sneezes once,
Or doesn't eat his food
You don't take bets! Straight to the vets!
We'll take no chances. Dude!

Just once, if lying with a cold,
Or feeling really very old
Or dying with a raging thirst,
It would be nice to be the first!

Before that 'Cooking Fat'!

Martin Buckley

THOUGHTS FOR THE SEASON - SUMMER

Summer is almost here
I hope it's not hot
But with climatic changes
Most definitely not
Weather will be sweltering
Need ice upon our seat
Pavements maybe melting
Right below our feet
Also on the uptake
Will need ice cream from vans
No not in say cornets
But the use of giant cans.

M D Bedford

SUMMER

There goes the deer
Jumping our gate.
Maybe they will soon find a mate.
We must make haste
I have got a date
Cat to the vet
She will scratch him I bet
Breakfast to make
How can I wait
I must away to start the day
The birds await their table store
I have given them seed and bread galore.

K Forcey

LITTLE DOG LOST
(Dedicated to Cally, my little love)

I remember the ways of your puppyhood days
Wagging tail and bright eyes that would shine
Gambolling round me - so ready for fun
You dear little pal of mine

You obeyed me, and gave all the love you could give
Your faithfulness showed - oh so clear
When I softly whispered - 'chocolate' or 'walks'
I could guarantee that you would hear

But now you are old - you won't do as you're told
I call - and my voice you ignore
I tell you to stay and you come anyway
You just won't obey anymore

But I love you my pet - so we go to the vet
Who says that the reason is clear
You are deaf, he is sure - and can hear me no more
And down my cheek courses a tear

For the old days I yearn but together we learn
For we have a love which can't end
For wherever I go, you're beside me and so
You're my shadow - my joy - my best friend

You're still dearer to me - as you sit on my knee
And I hug you - while I count the cost
That you who gave all - as you ran to my call
In a silent world - are a *little dog lost.*

Irene Beattie

Pussy Cat

Go cat, go and get it now
Knock over the vases and give a miaow
Sprinkle the carpet and scratch all the floor
Make a loud noise, 'til she opens the door

Pull all her wool and make a real mess
Leave it untidy, and she'll never guess
Lie on the bed, and make out you're asleep
When she comes in, take a wee peep

See if she's angry, or just simply mad
I am not naughty, I am real bad
I'll hide in the cupboard and snuggle up fast
Hoping quite soon, that the moment will pass

And maybe time later, when she has calmed down
I'll go for my food and I'll wander to town
Until she's cooled her mood, I'll keep out her way
And maybe tomorrow, I'll find wool to play

All over the house, I'll wind wool around
When she's asleep and not making a sound
'Cause she'll never hear me, I'll make sure of that
After all, what am I, I'm only a cat.

V J Haynes

A Resident's Tail

There was a mouse
That dared to live within my house.
There was a cat,
Well fancy that,
That spied the mouse
Inside the house.
The cat crouched low
(she wasn't slow)
And switched her tail.
The mouse turned pale
Ran back inside
Its hole to hide.
The cat went splat
Its face quite flat
Against the wall.
The mouse, so small
Could not recall
A cat so fast.
And so, at last,
Its nerves to soothe
It packed to move
And left its home
Prepared to roam.
There was a dog
Within the house
That spied the cat
That chased the mouse.

And, full of joy
With this new toy
The dog it pounced,
The cat it bounced,
The mouse it fled
Back to its bed.
And so all three
Still live with me.

Barbara Dunning

THE HORSE

Horses are fast and wild
Horses are graceful and strong
Horses mean power and strength to us
And our love for them lasts ever long

They're flighty and quick off the mark
But gentle and kind to us too
We treat them like one of the family
And that bond no one can undo

Our love for them comes from the heart
Some even may say from the soul
When man and his horse are together
They are not two but one whole

This affinity with horses will last
Forever and ever I'm sure
I will never stop loving my first two
Just more and more and more.

Olivia Kim Ruth King-Cook

MY DOG LUCKY

A soft fur coat
A big pink tongue
She always knew
When she'd done wrong.
Her wagging tail
And genuine smile
Kept us happy
For a while.
She loved the water
When going on a walk
Her friendly ways
Made her talk.
A happy dog
Healthy and fit
I would love to see
Her for a bit.
I miss the walks
Her friendly face
Now she's in another place.
Memories of Lucky
Will always stay
In my heart
I'll always pray
To see her again,
Just one more time
I'll never forget
A dog so fine.

Rachel Gallagher

A Dolphin's Life For Me

I'd like to be a dolphin
Far out, in the sea.
A dolphin's life, I'd like to have
So pure, tranquillity.

I'd glide through the water
And splash my tail about,
Dive down to see the coral,
Then come up, and jump right out.

I'd shout to all the fishermen,
As they came sailing by.
They'd watch me swimming along side,
Then watch me jump up high.

I'd see so many things
That live in the sea,
Like seaweed, and the coral
The odd shark, coming after me.

I wouldn't have to worry
As food goes swimming by.
And if I did feel lonely,
I'd give out a dolphin cry.

I wish I was a dolphin,
A life of play and sea.
But I'm a little girl,
Named Carla, that's me.

Mandy Craven

THE KINGFISHER

For the twitcher
There's no greater sight
Than to catch the kingfisher in flight

Majestic blue with chestnut breast
His beauty stands above the rest
Mother Nature's flawless dream
He dips and skims across the stream

And should the sunlight catch him right
No other bird appears so bright
Then perched on willow
Patience keen
With one sure dive
His catch is clean

The master angler takes his prize
And if good fortune deems you see
This spectacle before your eyes
Then be steadfast
Make sure you glance
To miss him means no second chance

Once more he's gone again in flight
For someone else to catch his sight.

Steven Krzymowski

I Am A Cat

I am a cat. I need to purr.
I need for you to stroke my fur.
I meet you on a time or two,
Present myself, my whole to you,
Desiring that you see in me . . .
This I suggest . . . do you agree
Without me telling you with voice?
I wish for it to be your choice,
To understand and know my need
And realise that in my greed
I love your touch, the warmth you give
That helps me better so to live.
This is the thought that I require
From you . . . to recognise desire
Without me having to explain,
For it's your love that keeps me sane,
I am a cat and I love you!

Joan E Blissett

BARNEY - A TRIBUTE

There will never be another Barney
Barney was everybody's friend
He gave a lifetime of devotion
Loyal and protective to the end.
On the day we first met Barney
He took to us from the start
And we fell in love with Barney
And he captured all our hearts.
He could sound so fierce could Barney
He would bark and make a din
And yet our little baby kitten
Was seen nestling 'neath his chin.
He went missing one day, Barney
We searched one cold and misty night
Head trapped in a snare, we found him
Cruel wire round his neck so tight
He gave us such a welcome, Barney
When released him from the wire
How he jumped for joy and licked us
Then home to warm milk by the fire.
But the years caught up with Barney
Oh! and how it broke our hearts
To see the pain, in his sad old eyes
The time had come for us to part.
By the roses we have buried Barney
Your resting place we'll always tend
You gave a lifetime of devotion
Sleep well, Barney old friend.

Pat Gooding

Paunce's Poem

Paunce is on his boiler, and a thousand purrs away,
    (Pauncey art thou sleeping thereupon?)
Stretched beneath the tea towels, below the mantelshelf,
    And dreaming all the time of Avalon.
Overhead the Munchies, over there the milk,
    And doggie ones awaiting, woebegone,
With the catflap rattling, with the night wind battling,
    He sleeps and waits for Whiskas when the morning comes anon.

Jo Brookes

OUR PET

Hilda is a hamster
Our furry little friend
When we let her out to play
The laughter never ends.

Christina loved her hamster
This little furry pet
One day she looked poorly
We took her to the vet.

But then on Thursday morning
When I came down the stairs
Hilda in her sleeping room
Just didn't seem aware.

Our lovely little furry friend
Her head laid on one side
Curled up that night and died.

Caroline Halliday

SUMMER IS A-COMING IN

Summer is a-coming in
With its magnificent array of colourful blooms
Gardens filled with lavish scents
Of flowers in borders and circular spreads
The trees fully awake with their fruit in full swing
And roads and hedgerows with flowers at their best,
                              brightening our way
Picnics galore are enjoyed in the country
Waterways sing merrily as they go on their way
The corn is ripe and full of joyful anticipation
Oh! Summer is a-coming in
Full of gladness and heartfelt joy.

Alma Montgomery Frank

THE SEASONS

Spring when it comes gives us much joy
if we are a girl or a boy
the flowers are showing their heads
in a lot of the flowerbeds.

Now we know summer won't be long anyway
it's certainly getting warmer every day
when summer's here the garden will bloom
and the lovely fruit will be ripe real soon.

We look forward to the fruit anyway
plums, pears, apples are a joy any day
strawberries, raspberries we had anyway
and didn't we enjoy them every day.

Then it's autumn, time to get ready for winter they say
it certainly gets cooler every day anyway
the fruit in the trees we can pick any day
the plums are delicious anyway.

Then it's winter that comes next anyway
we must realise it's colder every day
it's certainly cold we know
maybe we will soon have snow.

So the four seasons affect us in every way
when spring arrives we jump in joy anyway
summer we enjoy if a girl or boy
then when autumn comes we can do the same
we all know winter is coming again.

The seasons can give us joy any day
whatever we do, whatever we say
the whole year gives pleasure to us every day
even though it alters in so many ways.

K Taylor

GREEN HILLS

The long green hill, but is it?
How many greens are there?
Trees and grass, even brown twigs
In winter twigs are bare

The grass is a brightish green
The bushes are darker
Other colours may join in
And make a good marker.

Trees are very light in spring
Get dark as the year grows
Many greens appear later
They change as water flows.

We see these changes each day
When we are near the hill
Their beauty never leaves us
And is always a thrill.

Green, so many shades are here
Uncountable through change
So lovely to watch every day
To see God rearrange.

Edith Buckeridge

BRIGHT AUTUMN'S PANTRY

As the crisp golden leaves fall over the ground,
Near berries of hawthorn, red, shiny and round.
Tall trees above hold nests, empty and bare,
Fledglings, long gone, when the weather was fair.

Rich autumn has crept in, not making a noise,
Bright dressed in her brilliance and keeping her poise.
She's painted the leaves that have fallen around,
Then added a rustling and crackling sound.

Long woollen skirts gently swish through the leaves,
Making their way with such elegant ease.
This season of year has such treasures in store;
Fat plums and green apples and, oh, so much more.

Bright colours and berries, ripe fruit on the trees,
Abundance of life which is certain to please.
Sweet chutneys and pickles are now stored away,
Keeping their bounty for a cold winter's day.

Apples and pears rest on old wooden racks;
Potatoes, so cosy, in hessian sacks;
Fine bottles of wine are fermenting away
To make their appearance on next Christmas Day.

Gold autumn has lavished on us her bright best
And now is the time that she takes her long rest.
As the harshness of winter so soon will arrive,
Her gifts to our pantry make sure we'll survive.

Hazel Mills

SUMMER HOLIDAYS

We work all year to get the cash
Now this we can't afford
To take the kids on holiday
Make sure they don't get bored

There will always be a moment
When we hear that awful word
When our tempers rise within us
Oh how that word it hurts

They never stop to give a thought
How hard we have to save
To pay for all their luxuries
The food, the fun, the games

Now some day I know they'll understand
When they are adults too
How hard it's been to manage
School trips, their clothes, their food

So again it's time to hold our breath
Just hope they will enjoy
That the weather it is kind to us
The rain it stays away

The year's hard work is worth it
I am sure you will agree
Just to have a perfect holiday
Enjoyable and carefree.

Patricia McBride

OUR HOLIDAY

We went on a holiday to the Med,
One of three islands the brochure said.
The sun shone, it was lovely and hot,
Sitting round the pool really hit the spot.

St Paul's Bay's the place we stayed,
Next to Buggiba's blue sea.
Warm nights out for a meal,
Or under the palms for tea.

Buses go round the island,
In every direction, I'm told.
Mosta, Mdina and Marsaxlokk,
Are all good to behold.

Yes, Malta's the place we went,
The peoples most friendly by far.
It's easy to get to by air,
You can even go round it by car.

We'll go there again when we can,
After saving our pennies each week.
There's clean air, sea and sand,
And plenty of sun so to speak.

P R Baker

SUMMER

The morning sun shines through the tree
Their branches dance with the summer breeze
A bird sings from its highest limb
It stirs my soul from deep within

A snail moves through the dewy grass
A trail of silver left in its path
A spider climbs the mossy wall
A web of silk is its summer shawl

The gentle flow of a crystal stream
Its grassy bank like ribbons of green
The bird's song becomes a concert of sound
They sing in harmony from all around

I lie in the meadow in a sea of flowers
I look towards the brambles where a young rabbit cowers
I hear the sound of a bumblebee
I lie very still as it flies past me.

It's the season of joy that I dearly love
The gift we are given from the Lord above
It will all soon be over but I won't shed a tear
For we'll meet again this time next year.

Gareth Thorpe

SUMMER HOLIDAYS

Summertime is for fun and pleasure,
especially relaxing in nice warm weather,
it's holiday time, in the pool all day,
swimming along, not a care in the way,
getting a tan day by day
this is the life for me you say.
No cooking or cleaning that's what is best
just dressing up and dining out, that's what I call a rest,
dancing all night in the club,
it's better than being in the local pub,
the best holiday you've ever had
but it's time to go home and you feel really sad.
Travelling home thinking what you've done
the best time of your life, you've had so much fun,
you get home feeling exhausted after travelling all night,
the thought of going back next year, well maybe you might,
you reflect on the good times you have had
but back to reality the bank balance looks bad.

Linda Evans

HIDE AND GO SEEK
(Dedicated to the magic of autumn)

He's blown in again with his mellow brown bell
Old Father Autumn has cast oot his spell
On carpets of fallen leaves crunchy and brown
The children are playing on his golden gown

With a magical scarf that lights up her face
Pamela rolls in the sweet autumn race
Each season in turn will touch her fair hair
But autumn time tints shed light that is rare

One windy fresh night I rambled outside
The tints were so lovely on autumn's brown tide
Some children were playing at hide and go seek
In the soft autumn breeze I stopped for a peek

A group of young children danced round on the green
Pamela stopped and the yonkers were keen
Stay here by the tree with the ones that are het
Its branches will shelter you if it gets wet

I watched as the children played on in their game
Daniel spied Demi from hiding she came
You're caught you are het with Pamela stand
In the leaves of the tree was an autumn bird band

Blue-purple twilight fell down as I stood
The children played on through the enchanted wood
Bold autumn robins in cadence sang out
Their golden notes rang through the autumn about.

Roy A Millar

SUMMERTIME

It rained and rained and they wondered why
The wettest summer in years gone by
The usual suspects were called to bear
They blamed El Nino and the ozone layer
But a stranger truth was never told
To explain away the wet and cold
For far away an old warhorse
Defiantly stood against nature's force
And bellowing from a windswept scree
Repelled the waves of the raging sea.

Back they rolled from whence they came
Gathering cloud of hail and rain
To mightily crash on Europe's shore
With storm and flood and thunderous roar
And lest the sun should dare to play
A skyline cloaked with sheets of grey
Leaving neither rhyme nor reason
To justify the abject season
Except of course that distant soldier
Hollering from his lonely boulder.

R Burden

CRISPIN

I see the hazel catkins
Waving to and fro,
And underneath lies Crispin,
Why did he have to go?

Such a gorgeous creature
Loved sitting in the rain
Barely ten years old at that,
Why did he go - again?

Warts upon the ears had he,
I seem to watch them grow . . .
Vet said at once, 'It's cancer'
That's why he had to go.

I think he was just sent to me
His large green eyes aglow,
I'm sure he's happy where he is
Why did he have to go?

P Clinton

CATS IN SNOW

What's this?
What fun, this soft white stuff!
I jump!
Can't run - it's deep enough
To jump again, to chase my mate
With might and main, and find, too late

He's deep
Inside a strange white hole,
But he
Can't hide - and in I roll.
We pounce! It's cold! We shake our paws,
Then try to catch it with our claws.

We two,
We cats are having fun.
Such games!
The like we've never done
Before! We leap! What holes we make,
All white and deep, then try to take

Some
To share with those inside.
It's gone!
But where? Where does it hide?
Vanished quite - a mystery deep!
Ah, well - let's eat and wash, then sleep.

Margaret Ballard

OUR FOUR LEGGED FRIENDS

Heinz fifty-seven varieties
Our four legged friends
Faithful to the end.
Dogs have these similarities
All good owners' hearts they rend . . .

Ears alert, watchful,
Eyes see the key turn,
Legs bound up to welcome
Tongue licks in appreciation,
Much dedication.

Lesley J Worrall

THE GREAT BLUE FISH

There was an old lady, who had a great blue fish,
It swam down the stairs and landed in a dish,
In came the husband,
In came the maid,
In came the cook, who was brilliant at her trade,
The cook made a wish,
That cooked up a dish,
'Oh' said the lady,
'It was only a fish.'

L Howarth-Kirke

RIGSBY FAT CAT

He twitches his whiskers
And pricks up his ears;
He looks to the kitchen
As dinner time nears.
He bounds off the chair
His tail stands erect,
The clatter of dishes
Tells him what to expect.
Dear Rigsby, so friendly,
Your fur stripy clean,
No cat in the neighbourhood
Looks so serene.
We love your soft purr
As we tickle your chin;
And the way you patiently
Wait to come in.
But oh! You can't wait
To pinch the best seat,
He plays musical chairs
When you get up to eat.
You turn round to sit down
On what was your place,
And Rigsby is there . . .
He thinks your chair is ace!
He's the best, he's the boss,
So we have to give way
To the cat who is master
Of all we survey.

Evelyn Balmain

ANIMAL THOUGHTS

'There's going to be a referendum,'
Said the rabbit to the stoat.
'Then there'll be some changes
When I get my chance to vote.'

'I hadn't heard,' said Reynard fox,
While sitting on some logs.
'Does that mean I'll get a chance,
To chase those stupid dogs?'

'Will I get a bit of peace?'
Said the stag, up on the fell.
'The pink blackheads on horseback
Can make a stag's life hell.'

Pheasant in excitement clucked,
'With Grouse, I'll have a word.
I am just an immigrant
And he's a smart old bird.'

Grouse, Snipe and Woodcock,
At the prospect of some peace,
Happily put their names down,
Glorious twelfth would bring release.

Said a fat wood pigeon perched nearby,
Basking in the sun,
'The only time we'll get some peace
Is when we learn to fire a gun.'

Said Stoat, 'All very well but what of little me?
I am getting hungry,
Ask rabbit what's for tea.'

Derek B Hewertson

SAM

Loving eyes so full of trust,
Asking for a hug, that is a must.
No words does he convey.
But that is only his unique way.

A companion constant and sure.
Giving all and so much more.
A loyal friend that protects in the park.
Someone that makes me feel safe in the dark.

Handsome, strong, beautiful too.
Comes to my side when I put on a shoe.
Walks are an adventure as we reach the beck,
He stands smiling with water up to his neck.

No grumbles about diet, just fill up the dish.
Time is not important, just don't miss.
Words are inadequate, that is my folly,
When I describe Sam, our dog, the collie.

Mary Parker

MY LOVE OF THE SEA

A ripple of water,
The calm of the sea,
A mermaid of love,
For the world to see.

The sand on the beach,
So soft to the touch,
A magical place
It doesn't ask much.

Whales and dolphins
Ships of the night,
Filling our hearts,
With love, such a sight.

Full of romance,
From an unknown deep,
And now I close my eyes to sleep.

Deborah Coltman

THE SALMON

He thrushed his tail and took a leap
The spray went flying high
And from the depths of rocky bed
He got his glimpse of sky

Fish and falls fought the fight
And neither would unbend
But Nature knew what must be done
And where it all would end

So silver tail and flashing fin
Once more on rocks did fall
The salmon to the world would show
He'd answer Nature's call

The water foamed and torrent flowed
Like all that in Hell lies
And through the air as he made his leap
He heard the angler's sighs

Glistening rocks and sparkling spume
An arching, quivering streak
And to the pool that lay above
He landed safe but weak.

K K Work

THOUGHTS OF A SQUIRREL

I am a squirrel,
And my name is Cyril;
I don't gather nuts in May.
Though I've never bought 'em,
I get some in autumn
To feed me in winter - hooray!

I'm a squirrel, not squerril;
My mate's name is Meryl,
And both of us are coloured grey.
We've a son and a daughter,
Aged one and three quarters,
Or, rather, we had till that day.

Yes, we had a son
(He was our only one),
Who, I'm sorry to say, is now dead.
He was shot as a spy,
In the wink of an eye,
Because he was a Communist - red!

Although he was shot,
A traitor he's not,
So of him we are sadly bereft;
But one thing must be said:
Now that our son is dead,
There's more nuts for us three that are left!

Roger Williams

CATS

Gentle cuddly cats, green-eyed haughty cats,
Siamese with loud, yowling cries.
Yellow-eyed ginger cats, blue-eyed white cats,
Stealthily watching the skies.
No tailed, Manx cats, big fluffy grey cats,
Waiting to pounce on a bird,
Short haired tabby cats, marmalade mean cats,
Catching mice, without being heard!
Sleek, glossy cats, Burmese and blue cats,
Egyptians once thought cats were gods.
Disdainful, aloof cats, rat catching wild cats,
Surviving in packs 'gainst all odds!
Moggies, pet cats, spoilt pampered show cats,
Cushions all tattered and clawed,
Cute kittens, old cats, amusing, bold cats,
Every last one, is adored.
Mangy one-eared cats, ginger tom, feared cats,
Stealing fish from a pond.
Loveable, purring cats, black and white, 'talking' cats,
Anxiously, forging a bond!
Farm cats or family cats, silk coated, slinky cats,
We just love them all, we've been conned!

E M Eagle

WHITEY

It's a hard life being a hamster
You think I'm asleep, but I'm just resting my eyes
And planning what you humans can do for me
Keeping me fed and watered and cleaning out my cage
Oh, do I have to come out and play?
I'm a bit sleepy for your game
So I'll just curl up in my bedding
Besides, I'm dreaming a lovely dream
I'm Whitey, the cuddly super hamster
Sending you my love while I'm resting
It's a hard life being a wonder hamster

Neil Mason

LADY - MY OLD DOG

I look in your sad old eyes
I know the time is getting near
When you will be too weak and weary
To open those big brown eyes
You struggle to walk
You're weak at the knees
Your coat is thin, and
You have bad skin
But my darling border collie
You're faithful and loving still
You enjoyed your holiday
Even though so ill.

Linda Ann Marriott

OLIVER KITTEN

I found your photograph the other day
Your face was white and strained
I knew you were unhappy
That you did not want to say

I guess I was seven or eight-years-old
You my kitten, my wild feral kitten
With your Hitler-look moustache
So timid yet so bold

We loved one another so much
I had forgotten that
Until I saw your photograph

We all were glad you stayed
That you did not run away
Because you were my darling pussy cat

Susan Lewis

A Puppy's Tale

Our little eyes stared out of the box
Photos they promised to send
Saying they'd keep us together
Until the very end

We gave them all our love
And did as we were told
When we burned six months
They decided we must be sold

We didn't understand what was happening
When people with children came
They didn't want my brother Scruffy
He'd hurt his leg and went lame

They dragged me out of the door
But I didn't want to leave
And loaded me in a car
Then my brother was left to grieve

For many nights I lay awake
Then cried myself to sleep
Wondering where my brother was
And my best friend called Phillip

So when you see a puppy there
All cuddly, cute and sweet
Realise he's with you for life
And your friendship you can keep

Julie Hampson

THE STARE

As he stares at me from his favourite chair,
I wonder what he's thinking, from over there.
He doesn't blink or move his head,
Can't be hungry, he's just been fed.
It's not the first time he's stared me out,
I would just like to know what it's all about!
Perhaps he thinks, 'Why is she watching TV?
She should be over here, talking to me.'
They'll win me over, those staring eyes,
I start to laugh, and let out some cries.
He *still* hasn't moved, I can stand it no more,
I'm laughing so much, the tears start to pour.
Now, this beautiful cat, who I love to bits
Is looking so serious, and I am in fits!
The more I laugh, the harder the look
And I hide my face behind a book . . .
Sadly, he's no longer with me to play that game,
My very dear friend is a picture in a frame.
Sometimes, when I look at his empty chair,
I have to smile, as I remember that stare.

Jeannette Kelly

MY DOG

My dog is just a little pup,
For it's breakfast milk does sup.
It romps and plays around all day,
Then in my arms it will lay.

When I shout her for a game,
I call her Susie, that's her name.
She runs along so quick and free,
Chases cats up a tree.

Susie is so happy when in the wood,
I train her how to be good.
Not to chase after every rabbit,
For it is a very naughty habit.

When it's time she wants feeding,
Or something else she is needing.
She licks my face and my hand,
Cocks her head and looks grand.

Every day we have such fun,
Playing outside in the sun.
She's quite happy with a ball,
When I kick it against the wall.

She runs and chases it around,
Then falls over on the ground.
Tired out, she lays down in a heap,
Closes her eyes and goes to sleep.

Her day is over and so to bed,
To rest her very weary head.
She played all day, till the night,
So now I'll turn out Susie's light.

D Kirk

My Cats

Must write about them before
they fade into the memory bank.
Such pranks, such joys, delightful
things, I have my cats to thank.
I have photos of my last four cats
on the mantelpiece neatly framed.
Have a memorial gravestone in the
garden and all are named.

What good times I had when I had
the pleasure of their company.
They all had different characters,
and a spirit that was free.
All lived to a ripe old age,
can be thankful for that.
I do miss the valued company
of my darling pussycat.

I loved them all dearly, and
dealt with problems one at a time.
Looking back, not much was wrong,
most things were just sublime.
The memories of their lives are
still very clear to me, so
can still shed a tear for a cat
that died over 40 years ago.

Ann May Wallace

SANDY MAC'TAVISH

Given to me as a pup
When we lived abroad,
By Mac'Tavish . . . Father's friend;
I at four adored
The rough haired friend with four legs
And docked stumpy tail.
They asked me what I'd call him,
Saying he was male.
Putting him down by my feet,
He dug in the sand.
His coat matched the golden beach,
I took Father's hand.
'He is Sandy Mac'Tavish . . .
That will be his name.'
So we grew up together,
He played many games.
He lived till he was 18.
I at 22
Had lost my trusted best friend:
Best friends are so few.
I smile when I remember
How he guarded me.
Anyone not known to him
I could guarantee,
Heard his growl and saw his teeth;
So would keep away.
If they sat down or near me,
'Tween us he would lay.
Watchful ever vigilant
I love him to this day.

Elwynne

FLOWERS

What would life be without flowers
For happy occasion or sad
Flowers to greet a new baby
Congratulations to new mum and dad
Flowers for birthdays - a lovely bouquet
Or a single red rose on a special day
Flowers for a bride as she walks down the aisle
With beauty and grace and elegant style
Flowers to cheer a down-hearted friend
To help mend broken hearts when relationships end
Flowers for folk who are suffering and ill
To comfort and help them over the hill
Flowers for people whose life's at an end
Flowers in bereavement condolence to send

Dorothy Margaret Smith

THE EAGLE AND HIS MATE

The eagle, he sits on the cliff tops high
Looking about him with taleful eye
He is standing like a sentry guarding the world
Above his beautiful head his mate twists and twirls
She is searching for a place to build her nest
While her lord and master takes a well-earned rest
He had been searching since early morning light
To find a place that was just *right*
This was first time at mating and building
He wanted it good for his chosen so loving
He stretched his huge wings, shook his shaggy head
Took off with a cry that could be heard ringing
Way up into the sky white with clouds drifted as the wind blew
Seemed to soar with him as he flew higher and higher
Calling to his mate, to match him in her flight
She twisted and twirled matching his antics at each turn
And seemed to meet in midair their beaks to touch
As if they kissed then turned away, flying higher and higher in play
Suddenly he swooped straight down into the canyon far below
Something he had spotted glistening in the snow
Bones that had been left, sun and rain had turned them to a white bleach
He hovered awhile then flew straight down
Picked some up in his strong beak
Took off again with the wind in his wings
Straight to the cliff top and dropped these things
At the feet of his loved one who stood patiently by
She gazed at them awhile then placed them one by one
On top of the wood she had already moved
So it went on for most of the day
Building then resting, flying at a very fast pace
Night began to fall, the scent of pines filled the air
The two golden eagles so much in love
Guarding their nest on the cliff top above

God was in his Heaven, they were in theirs
Midst the humming mosquitoes and whispering firs
They will continue with their lives
Hatching their family - so busy will they be
So ends my little story.

Irene Hartley

Night Sky

Night sky, pink clouds gently drifting by,
Golden sun slowly sinking in the pink-blue sky.
Night clouds gathering, glimpsing the moon,
Casting shadows as darkness looms.
Black velvet sky studded with stars,
Sending forth their light from afar.
Early dawn mists rolling over the land,
Shrouding the sea and the sand.
The foghorn sounding out a warning,
On this foggy, misty morning.
Spider's webs sprinkled with early morning dew,
Like shimmering diamonds for all to view.

Zoiyar

NATURE

Now that summer months are here, once again
Away from spring, and the light rain
When once the showers, came falling down
Yet, bringing the beauty, clad in nature's gown

When the loveliest of trees, blow to and fro
Where the peace of the rivers, gently flow
Which offers us hope, and peaceful bliss
While, the love birds, steal their loving kiss

Oh, such a contrast, that summer does hold
When Mother Nature brings back, the wealth of gold
Covering the countryside, with different flowers
Throughout the wonders, of these shining hours

While, the blackbirds' notes are so full of cheer
The swallows' strong wings, flutter so near
Listening to their twittering notes, produced on their wings
Flying through the air, catching insects, for their offspring

The swift flies by, and shrills, a far carrying scream
Spoiling the peace, of a lovely summer's dream
Soon, their fast beating wings glide over their nesting colony
Feeding their young ones, till the chicks fly off, independently

Such loveliness is in view, through the summertime
When birds sing their different notes, of rhythm and rhyme
Where the lovely trees hang in full bloom, on their bough
Whispering to the gentle breeze, where the rivers flow

When day is done, birds nestle, when twilight appears
Just leaving the sounds, from the sweet nightingales' cheers
A variety remarkable rich notes are heard, and a lullaby
Perhaps chirping to the birds, resting on the tree tops high

Thank God for all the nature, and the birds of the air
Through the magical hours, that we may hear and share

Jean P McGovern

Summer Evening Magic

Still, motionless the evening air.
No cooling breeze, no sound to share.
Slowly fading into night,
The shadows lengthen, without light.

Gnats, flitting in a glorious dance,
Rise and fall, as in a trance.
A ballet of a myriad wings,
Still to daylight's dance they cling.

Soon, shadows cross the face of all,
Surrender to the cold night fall.
Flowers dip their heads in sleep,
Moon and stars come out to peep.

A harvest moon hides behind the trees,
Like patterned lace, through a veil of leaves.
A velvet sky, lit now with beams,
Casts its spell, and all the garden dreams.

Gwyneth Pritchard

MY DOG JAX
(To Natalie)

When I think back about my dog
Twelve stone of him, built like a log
He was faithful, his name was Jax
Oh, he was company, helping me to relax
Such a loving dog he was to me
Trouble was he always rolled in the pigeries
Very dirty, smelly walking down the path
Just had to put him in the bath
Loved him so much, just couldn't get cross
Knowing when he died, he was one great loss
Thinking about him day by day
Such a faithful dog, always got his way
A dog is for life that's true
Oh Jax, I do miss you
My golden retriever was the love of my life
Still got his name plate, and send my love to him each night

    God bless you Jax, miss you so very much

Anne Davey

HOUDINI

I have a little rabbit,
I call him Mister Harry,
He keeps escaping from his cage,
To play at catch and carry.

It's really quite annoying,
As he does it quite a lot
And if he does one more time,
I fear Harry is going in the pot!

He runs through all the gardens,
He frolics in the grass
And if I can get just close enough
He will be in for an early bath.

A dart! A dash! Alas I missed
And off he goes again,
I fear my little furry friend
Is becoming quite a pain.

Well now if I'm really honest
And to you I will admit
That if he really ran away
I would miss him quite a bit!

John Green

THE ELEPHANT

Why do I like the elephant? Not pretty, not at all,
It's much too big and dirty grey with eyes that are too small.
The ears are just like cabbage leaves, the tail not worth attention,
The feet are flat with wrinkly legs but the trunk is worth a mention.

Molly Phasey

Two Pets

My dog is playing in the snow.
The wind by the barn's making fru.
The kitten's skipping to and fro.

I threw a stick - not to a foe.
It was a gift to my friends true.
My dog is playing in the snow.

The dog he loves to make a show.
The landscape is a pleasant view.
The kitten's skipping to and fro.

Strong and healthy the two will grow.
Abide they must to see life through.
My dog is playing in the snow.

One day the dog away must go.
The kitten will be all askew.
The kitten's skipping to and fro.

Death's always in the wings you know.
Long life is given to a few.
My dog is playing in the snow.
The kitten's skipping to and fro.

Angus Richmond

THE SHADE

On the brow of a distant hill,
    Stands the pale shape of a tree -
And the night wind sends sad music,
    Down gently to me.

Its form is small and gnarled,
    A dead thing, forlorn.
And it stands where once
    A precious dream was born.

For something less than a shade,
    Haunts me far and long,
With the faint, summery breath,
    Of a half-forgotten song.

And naught but a vast sorrow,
    Abides in the craggy dales,
And treads in breathless silence,
    The verdurant, wooded vales.

And in the dappled, fading light,
    The lost and fair,
Waits, and a lone shadow leans,
    In dreaming despair.

Derek Budd

DIGGING

'Come out and dig your garden,'
The blackbird sang to me.
'I've heard some worms a-moving
Under the gooseberry tee.
My wife is now a-sitting on her
Eggs, two or three,
And she's sent me collectin'
Worms to feed her - see?'

'Come out into the garden,'
The robin said, 'Encore,
My wife is sitting on her eggs
And can't get out no more.
She wants those nice white grubs
You find, and centipedes galore.
The transport is my business,
But diggin' is your chore.'

'Get out and dig the garden,'
My good wife ordered me.
'You haven't set a single spud
Or sown a bean or pea.
I spend an awful lot upon green grocery
And what's grown in the garden
I always get for free.'

I don't care what the blackbird sings
Nor what the robin said,
And much of what my good wife says
Goes in and out my head.
I won't be driven to gardenin'
All right, I can be led!

Walter Dalton

NORFOLK PIGS

Why was I ever born? So oft have heard folks say,
But do you often wonder, with pigs out on display
In Norfolk fields getting fatter, boars and their chatter
Little ones all around, after giving Mum pig a smacker.

Why was I ever born? Perhaps those young pigs say
As they all munch and chatter, appear happy and gay.
Does their mum ever tell them, as ours often do we :
You are really for providing ham child, for the humans' tea.

Or roast pork for their dinners, so they too can stuff,
Although not in muddy Norfolk fields, neat bluff.
At their dinner tables, with stuffing and the rest,
Perhaps it's better you do not know, all the rest,
    You're blessed!

Geoffrey S Wilyman

My Dog

My dog is black with a white-tipped tail,
He jumps up to greet me each day without fail.
He is strong and bouncy and loves his walks,
At times he whimpers and almost talks.

I brush him and comb him till his coat shines,
And when I'm away, I'm sure he pines.
He knows too, whether I'm happy or sad,
He can change my mood to good from bad.

Without him there to encourage me on,
I would flounder and fail, all hope gone.
His trust in me, his fun and grace,
Keep me strong, healthy, and in my place!

S J Dodwell

SUNNY

There's a King Charles spaniel I know called Sunny
The things he gets up to are sometimes quite funny.
He stays with his owner, when out on his lead
And when he goes home he will look for his feed.
He's good with the children, wherever he goes
And his ears are so droopy, they cover his toes.
He's loved by his mum and he goes up to bed
Last thing at night after he's been fed.
On dull days and grey days, he will not play games
But on nice sunny days, he lives up to his name.

B Smith

A Dog's Prayer

A comfy bed by the fire, or somewhere
    draught free, that'll do nicely.

Toys to play with, food and treats
    and I'll be your friend for life, you'll see.

Take me on walks every day in woods,
    with exciting smells and new places to explore,

Meeting up with doggie pals, chasing rabbits
    and birds together, I could ask for nothing more.

If I'm lucky, a roll in dead frog, or decomposed mouse,
    to me would be an utter delight.

Better still, a quick dive into a muddy stagnant pond,
    emerging all slimy and looking an absolute fright!

A kind, caring, considerate owner, who understands
    that a dog needs these simple pleasures.

In return for all these things, I'll protect your family
    and home and become such a beloved treasure.

I'll learn to come back on the lead when commanded
    and I promise not to roam far from you.

I'll lick your face, ears, in fact everywhere,
    to show you how much I care for and love you.

When the postman pushes the mail through the letter box,
    I'll try not to snatch them from his hand,

And chew them up before you've time to read them,
    because I'll soon understand,

That we dogs have to adapt to your way of life,
    if we're to share your world with you.

In return we'll be warm, fed, well cared for,
    so loved and cherished too.

Dot Ridings

THE SHELTIE

Our dog it was a Sheltie
Cluny was his name
He wasn't kept for hunting
Rabbit, grouse or game
He was just our pet
Timid and not sure
Of anyone but us
Who came calling at the door

His coat was brown and sable
His paws a snowy-white
Brushed and groomed
He was such a bonnie sight
He was never any trouble
Always there when you did call
Following you around the house
Or chasing his wee ball

Alas! Our Sheltie he took ill
But not once did he complain
Although the vet assured us
He must have been in pain
The kindest thing that we could do
Was put our pet to sleep
Now we have just the memory
Of the pet we used to keep

Peter P Gear

REFLECTIONS

There's a strange creature looking at me,
Through the big glass door,
He's brown, like me, with fluffy ears,
And sitting on the floor . . .
When I look left,
He looks left,
When I bow,
He does that too,
His tail is wagging,
Same as mine,
Mum, what can I do?
If I bark,
He echoes back,
He's beckoning to me too,
I'd really like to play with him,
Can I go outside too?
Strange, there's no one out here now,
Seems he's gone away,
I'll come back in and play with you,
My friend can't want to play.
The door's now shut,
I'll go and look . . .
There's a strange creature looking at me,
Through the big glass door,
He's brown, like me, with fluffy ears,
And sitting on the floor!

Lynda Burton

CATS

I love my little pussycats
They're all about my room
They're big and small - I love them all
They make my heart just zoom.

The family say, 'Get rid of them
They just collect the dust'
But I just say that they will stay
So why make such a fuss?

They do not eat. They do not drink
They always look so funny
They fill me full of happiness
And don't cost a lot of money.

Everyone must have a fad
And pussycats are mine
I know they do not make *you* glad
But to me they are just fine.

The dear old cats don't mess about
They cannot run around
You never, never hear them shout
With goodwill they abound.

Why is my heart so full of gloom?
As I look around my room
It's that space upon the mat
Oh heck! They've pinched a little cat.

D Adams

SECRET LOVE

I wake up startled in the gloom
And find him standing in my room.
Doesn't say a word, just sits on a chair
And tells me how lucky I am that he is there.
Says don't make a noise, don't make a fuss,
This is a secret between the two of us.
Telling me it's right, so just pretend,
What can I do? He is Dad's best friend.

When he is gone, I go back to sleep,
This is a terrible secret to keep.
But who would believe the words of a child like me?
So I just smile secretly.
I wouldn't want to sleep in a kennel, on my own,
He is only a puppy, time enough for that when he is grown.

Maureen Arnold

THE JOYS OF GETTING OLD

Oh what a life, I often say,
Cause you get a lot of problems when you're old and grey.
I'm over 60 you see, and they say I'm no good,
But I'll prove them so wrong - if only I could!
No one will employ me, it does seem a shame,
I can't get a job, my age is to blame.
Alone in my room, I think of the past,
How things used to be, and why they didn't last.
I look in the mirror and what do I see?
A poor reflection of how I used to be.
My face is full of wrinkles, my hair is going thin,
I'm losing my sight, while gaining another chin.
My stomach is bloated, and my ego is dented,
I get no fulfilment, because I'm never contented.
Voices in my head, shingles in my leg, carbuncles above the knee,
That hurt so much at the slightest touch,
Yes it's so good when you reach 60.
I was known as a Casanova, but the years have cramped my style,
With me aches and pains and varicose veins, I can't even raise a smile.
I tried some of that Viagra, but it didn't do the trick,
Me *neck* went all stiff and swollen, *not* me dangly bit.
I'm hard of hearing, and blind in one eye,
And I fall of my bike, when I give it a try.
I walk with a limp, and use a white stick,
I talk to myself - it helps quite a bit.
Pains in my back, cause me much grief,
But a young woman's soft touch would be such a relief.
So I must stay in control, for there's too much at stake,
Cause if I get any worse, I might jump in the lake.

Brian Lorkin

PUPPY LOVE

I woke up one morning, all cold, snowy and dark,
Oh the little darling, I heard a puppy bark.
I went downstairs and opened the door wondering what I might find,
When out of the blue a bundle of fluff came running round behind.
I bent down, picked him up, didn't hesitate to take him in,
I feed him, cuddled him, and thought oh what a sin.
I wonder where he's come from had someone put him out?
I know this does happen - I'd like to try and find out.
I made a few enquiries, reluctant to give him up,
But had someone somewhere genuinely lost a little pup?
I'll make some more enquiries, just maybe two or three,
All the time thinking, he'd be better off with me.
The weeks have past, the months have too,
He's growing all the time,
If anyone was to ask me now, I'd say, yes he's mine.
He's a joy to have, a little love and as happy as can be,
I told you how the months have flown,
He's just coming up to three.

A J Witherington

The Butterfly

While sitting in my garden, which I call paradise
I gazed upon something that was beautiful and nice
It was a butterfly I spotted from up in the sky, it was one of God's
                                                            beautiful creatures
Its wings were white with little brown specks
As it moved it looked stunning with special effects
It liked my garden of so many bright colours
But its favourite was to like to red flowers
It fluttered around there for hours and hours
It was so lovely to gaze upon its beauty
While it was gently fluttering around doings its duty
Every move it made as it fluttered by
Was soft and gently as a sigh
That butterfly is welcome in my garden of paradise, it can visit any time
Cause to gaze upon its beauty is really quite divine

Toni Attew

GARDENING

Who loves gardening?
I do, I do, I do
Throughout all the seasons
My love remains always true
All through the wintertime, many plants sleep
Awaiting in their own time; through the garden to peep
Mother Nature keeps for us, colour all around
Whilst some trees sleep, they have patterns to show
And the beauty of evergreens contrast the beauty of snow
Branches laden in crystal white
They show contrast of silvery light
The red of the berries for seasonal cheer
Until we pass into another new year
Then through the ground a gradual peep
The snowdrops appear after a long sleep
Even with Jack Frost o'er the ground
They show no fear, there they abound
Trumpeting next, the daffodils gay
They sway in the wind as if to say
'Spring is coming, hooray, hooray'
Spring when Mother Nature will renew
The plants we all love to be anew
Each day in the garden, we take a peep
To see and delight those awakening their sleep
And how they have multiplied down in the deep
Peeps of delight day by day
To tell us once more
That spring's on its way.

Thelma Jean Cossham Everett

DESPONDENT AUTUMN

The Earth looks dull and tired
After a summer of incessant rain.
More sunshine really is required
To yield up crops of golden grain.
The farmers now are in a hurry
To gather in the straggling bales of hay.
A 'falling glass' adds to the worry
Of livestock prices tumbling day by day.

Skeins of wild geese in Vs across the sky,
Honking noisily, 'Which way, which way?'
Swallows head off for climates warm and dry;
Only the robin and the sparrows stay.
Wayside grasses, once so green and tall,
Now brown and drab against the wall.
Tree leaves hang mildewed over all
Awaiting the pyrotechnic hues of fall.

Soon farmyard beasts will be installed in byres.
The air is filled with reek from household fires.
The yearly contract to humanity expires,
And Mother Earth to slumber now retires.
In spring she'll rise up once again,
Her face refreshed by soft cool rain.
The wind blows cobwebs from her eyes,
Warmed by sunshine, glowing from the skies.
She'll start the cycle of fertility once more,
To feed her children as before.

A Gwynn

SEEDS OF LIFE

Fields of acorns scattered free
Many share their life with thee
Those embedded, breaking through
As nature's cycle starts anew.

They stretch and grow to endless height
Exaggerate their endless plight
Expanding arms embrace the world
So proud they stand with leaves unfurled.

See what glory can be grown
When nature's chosen seeds are sown
First the acorn, then the tree
Then the vast green forestry.

Give a thought, act a deed
Then you can sow a worthy seed
See its impact, rippling far
Like the trail of a shooting star

Turn to nature, hear it teach
Man its pupil, wind its speech
Prioritise, let go, be free
Help man to change his destiny

Live life simply, understand
Respect your neighbour, love the land
Walk together, side by side
Let nature be your humble guide

Pam Samways

FOOT AND MOUTH, 2001

The countryside is quiet and still
Death's hush over meadow and hill
Spread by anything that moves
Strikes animals with cloven hooves

Dairy cows' milk does disappear
With beef herds' meat inferior
It makes them all extremely ill
But foot and mouth it will not kill

To contain the disease, mass slaughter
None are spared, or given quarter
Carcasses piled on funeral pyre
Still cases rise higher, higher

Off bounds are the country walks
No one allowed into the parks
Straw disinfected bars the way
Even farm kids not out to play

When it gets warmer we'll be free
Once more to enjoy the country
Many a beast will have been slain
To make us virus free again

Winsome Mary Payter

THE TREE

The tree stands proud as it can be,
Its branches stretched out, swaying wild and free.
In the blowing winds both strong and calm,
Where the birds find shelter, away from all harm.
They sit close together, in all kinds of weather,
And converse with each other, in their own special way.
When they come for their food,
They're a cheerful brood,
With a pecking order, so the leader eats first.
But sometimes a bird, who thinks all this absurd,
Will try to come first, then confusion reigns,
Bringing anger and pain, with no better gain.
As the food spills over, falling down to the ground.

In our own family tree, the Tree of Mankind,
A haven to rest, away from all stress.
We all try to find, contentment of mind,
But we like the birds, sometimes like to come first.
And if it's not our turn, then resentment occurs.
So where there was peace, discontent is released,
Then the haven's a battlefield of our own making.
We've created disorder, because we are taking
Something that is not ours.

Yet we have the power to change all this.
To make in our hearts, a place of bliss.
And just like the birds, we too are free,
To enable our Tree, a haven to be.
So in taking our turn and thinking of others,
We can all live together, like sisters and brothers.
Then in doing our best wherever we can,
We'll stand proud like the Tree,
In the Family of Man.

Kathleen Rose Ferguson

Our 'Burmese' Dilemma

Our little Tommy Tucker, he really is a pain,
He rules the roost in our house and drives us all insane.
He brings us lots of presents and drops them at our feet,
A mouse, a vole, a squirrel and thinks it's such a treat.
He got onto the roof one night and cried with all his might,
I shouted, 'Oh! He's stuck, he's stuck,' he gave me such a fright.
Hubby in his nightshirt, got his long ladders out,
And gently brought him back to Earth (quite cross, without a doubt).
Tommy thought, this game's quite good, I'll lead them both a dance,
Then up the drainpipe disappeared, without a second glance.
He's not too sure about the dog next door, but answers Lucy's call,
Though Lucy's very, very big and Tommy's very small.
We tell him all our secrets and problems by the score,
He listens patiently, then purrs and lends a paw.
The children off our hands at last and worries almost gone,
But now we've got this blessed cat our loyalties are torn.
My bedding plants are dug up, as fast as they go in,
And dare the goldfish surface, he's waiting by the bin.
He stays away some evenings, and worries us no end,
Then crawls in on three legs next day quite unconcerned.
But would we do without this pet, this bundle cute and small?
We wouldn't change him for the world and love him faults and all.

Susan Carline

BUSTER

He's big and beautiful and black,
With white bits here and there.
He has a ring of confidence
Which makes him debonair.

His coat he washes twice a day
To keep it nice and slick.
Because there is so much to do
He soon runs out of lick.

To keep his form in perfect shape
He strolls across the lawn,
Or sits upon the garden seat
Where he can stretch and yawn.

He is an ornithologist
And likes to watch birds play,
But if they come too close to him
He looks the other way.

He's loveable and cuddlable,
There's nothing he likes more
To find a lap where he can nap
Until the day is o'er.

Patricia Biggs

GNASHER'S REVENGE

Gnasher is a wild, black cat
Who especially likes my goldfish.
That he would go and live elsewhere
Has to be my fondest wish.
I'm never cruel to this dumb beast
But then neither am I kind.
He prowls around our property
To see what he can find.

My wife asked me the other day
To take him to the vet;
'It seems his fur is falling out
And he's itchy, which makes him fret.'
The basket was prepared with care
To carry the pesky blighter.
'Come to Daddy, Gnasher dear.'
I couldn't have been politer.

As he tucked in, I took my chance
And grabbed him by the neck
To lift him in the basket. I cried,
'In you go!' 'In there? Like heck!'
And with a twist like a crocodile,
He sank his fangs into my finger.
He hissed and spat and cried like a fiend.
In the garden I would not linger.

And yet he would not release his grip,
He dug his teeth in deeper.
I whirled him round above my head
And threw him at the Virginia Creeper.
My blood began to pour from the wound,
The pain, like a red hot poker.
I ran inside, turned on the cold tap.
Bitten by a cat, what a choker!

After half an hour the bleeding slowed,
Becoming just a trickle.
I would gladly have chopped his tail right off,
If to hand there had been a sickle.
To the village nurse I had to go,
My finger wrapped in a towel.
'What have we here?' the nurse enquired,
As I tried my best not to howl.

'An anti-tetanus is what you need.
I'll also give you a dressing.
Take Panadol to ease the pain.'
At least that was a blessing.
She jabbed the needle in my arm;
The pain equalled that in my digit.
I squirmed and flinched and shouted, 'Ouch!'
The nurse said, 'Please don't fidget.'

I trundled home, tail 'tween my legs,
With injured finger, arm and pride.
I found Gnasher sitting there sunning himself -
He didn't even bother to hide.
I'll chase him off, next time I see him,
He's really had his chips.
But what was that I could see on his face?
A Cheshire Cat smile on his lips!

D J Jasper

CATS

Four-legged mammals covered in fur,
Pointed ears and the loudest purr,
Velvet ears and velvet nose,
Velvet chin and velvet toes -
    Cats.

The sweetest of faces with trusting eyes,
Thick, white whiskers and a yawn so wide,
Soft, furry tummies and soft, paddy paws -
Soft leather footpads - and sharp, painful claws!
    Cats!

All furry, appealing, most loveable pets,
Rubbing themselves cosily all around your legs;
They make themselves at home just anywhere,
Hiding in cupboards and under the stairs -
    Cats.

Preening and grooming, having a wash,
Balancing effortlessly on the narrowest ledge -
Then crouching, menacing, ready to pounce -
Gotcha! Look, I've just killed a mouse.
    Cats!

Miaow, purr, those are the sounds we hear,
Ah! Love 'em, the little dears.
Not so appealing when we hear a howl,
That means the lovelies are out on the prowl.
    Cats!

Kathy Rawstron

THE ISLAND OF SAMOS

Sparkling jewel in the eye of Turkey's crown
Straits of the seven stadiums stretching down
Toward a gentle cove of green and lapis blue
Footsteps on the beach left naked and anew
                     For me and you.

The glory of the sun through whispering tree
Drifting through your mind, the lapping sea
Visionary day-dreams in every varied hue
Your summer skies so unashamedly blue
                     For me and you.

Wandering from surf and stones you see
White-washed walls beneath a trailing tree
Pink petal glory flowers cascading into view
Shadow doors that open into deep Aegean blue
                     For me and you.

Jennifer H Fox

THE RIVER

As through shady glades you wander
On your journey to the sea
Think of tales that you could tell
And the sights that you have seen

Reflections from the sky above
Trees growing on your banks
Branches swaying, children playing
Meadows green and cornfields waving

Sweet music in the air
Sounds of church bells far away
Birds singing in the trees
Echoes on a summer breeze

As you wander on your way
Sweet the thoughts of happy days
Thinking of places you have been
On your journey to the sea.

Doreen Moscrop

WALK WITH ME

Walk with me, long golden pathways,
Across the fields, over the bridge.
Sunset dance on golden evenings,
Its curtain falls on distant ridge.
Walk with me through fields of clover,
Evening dew beneath our feet.
Be my warmth, as evening shrouds us
So not alone the night we greet.

Rachel Lowery

GREEDY CAT

The cat
sat
and ate the rat.

A fitting prize
for one who lies
and rakes the barn with golden eyes.

Patience pays
and skill always
the quarry captures.

Till torment o'er
and torture done
sees cat in raptures.

Gorging fur, crunching bone
a little meat to carry home
in swollen belly soft as silk.

To finish off - a drop of milk
provided by a little girl
who never knew about the kill.

Gail McClory

MY TORTOISE SNOOPY

I bought her when we were allowed to buy.
Before the ban, and the hue and cry.
When importing caused so many to die!

I can tell her off till I'm blue in the face,
And then she'll retreat in her carapace.
And comes out again at her own steady pace.
I'm sure she knows she's in disgrace!

She gets up in the morning and sits by the light.
Her head's alert and her eyes are bright.
She expects her food to be in her sight.
At least I know *she's* had a good night!

If the weather's poor, she'll sleep all day.
But if the sun shines, she'll wander away.
I talk to her often but she doesn't respond,
But I'm sure we have a sort of bond.
Two cranky oddballs I'm sure we are.
Who cares, she's always my shining star.

She's not a cuddly sort of pet.
She's hard and spiky, and can be wet.
I feed her well, she continues to grow.
Why tortoises appeal to me I do not know!

Some years she has laid a wonderful clutch.
But then the hatchlings have been too much
To look after and cope with from day to day.
I've had to send them on their way.

Still, I love her to bits, she's part of my scene.
Torts have come and gone but she's always been
That priceless pet who has a special place.
Hopefully, she'll outlive me given God's good grace.

Joan Edwards

ODE TO MY DOG

I've had you from three months old
And decided to call you Dudley
The reason for this is very obvious
It's because you are so cuddly.
We've had the good we've had the bad
We've had happiness and we have been sad
Your coat is cream and often curly
And I'm afraid you wake up early.
We've gone for walks and had some fun
Gone out in the winter and out in the sun
We've been together for many years
We've had our doubts and had our fears
You prefer a man I must say
I've always thought that you were gay
We'll carry on until the end, I fear
But with your deafness, you won't hear
I know I shall have you till the end
But does it matter you're my friend.

Eileen E Whittaker

'SOOTY' - A BELOVED CAT

One sunny day he came to stay,
A ragged and bedraggled stray,
We couldn't turn that cat away - 'our Sooty'.

One eye was bright and one was dim,
But he was sound of wind and limb,
We took him in and cared for him - 'our Sooty'.

We loved our black and gentle cat,
And people said, 'Well! Fancy that,'
He's really grown quite big and fat - 'your Sooty'.

I give my knee a little tap,
And he'll jump up upon my lap,
And settle down to have a nap - 'dear Sooty'.

He's very old - about 18,
And goodness knows just where he's been,
Up hill and mountain, dale and dene - 'has Sooty'.

He understands just what we say,
And he'll 'miaow' and talk all day,
I hope he *never* goes away - 'our Sooty'.

He eats his dinners without fail,
Then licks himself from ears to tail,
He's one of us - and *not* for sale - 'is Sooty'.

You're beautiful and soft my dear,
I hope you'll live for many a year,
But sadly not too more, I fear - 'Oh! Sooty'!

Avril T Hogg

CATS AND KITTENS

Cats and kittens, curled up tight, making miaows in the night
Cats and kittens, delightful to see, they should all be very free,
Cats and kittens, licking their coats, cuddly, lovely, they get my vote.
Cats and kittens, of all sorts of colours, some have a purr, others miaow.

Anna Parkhurst

HERBIE

Just above the ground you stand
but mighty, proud and strong,
ferocious teeth and gentle eyes
but boy! You don't half pong.

Protecting your own mistress well,
this sacrifice your vigil.
Intelligence your stronger point
until you want a widdle!

A broken coat and silky head -
with patches here and there.
Stealthily you'll sneak away but,
Herbie don't you dare!

As agile as those leaping cats
and spirited as the hawk.
My only true devoted friend
I wish you'd learn to talk.

Loyalty your middle name,
handsome, young and true.
Jack Russell would be proud of you -
A rascal through and through.

Amanda Richards

THE PHEASANT

The pheasant is a gaming bird and a table delicacy
Most rich landowners rear them for shooting down
It hailed from Eastern Europe and the Black Sea on the banks of the
river Puasis
Some say the Romans imparted them here, sometimes up in shops in
town

On the fields it is often seen picking in the soil for food
And its call can be heard among the woods and trees
Pheasants take off and fly from danger, in the wood
Shooting time is October until February that is when it's free

The cock bird is very colourful and its tail is very long
Some have a white collar above the neck a shade of blue
Its beak of white and its head is coloured by beautiful red crown
The hen is not as colourful as the cock bird gives its due

To the plainset of its coat of feathers of light brown
The beautiful copper plumage of the cock bird is a great sight
The nest is placed on the ground brambles, which have, overgrown
Up to ten to fifteen olive brown eggs are usually laid out of the light

R T Owen

MY CAT

My cat sits in the window
aloof and hard to please.
And gazes out in great disdain
upon the world she sees.
A purr, a sudden change of mood
she jumps upon my knee.
The kitten, still within the cat
the eyes say play with me.
I know I'll never own her
she stays to please herself.
But underneath that haughty gaze
her love means more than wealth.
So cat and dogs, together
each on their different way.
Bring laughter in our lives
and love along the way.

Gladys Mary Gayler

WALKING THE DOG

A walking in the woods we'll go, just me, my dog and I.
A walking in the woods we'll go; what, pray, will we espy?

We do not need conveyance, to reach the woodland rides,
For trees are clustered round our house, to front and back and sides.

Heading north's a downhill route, to vale of fern and willow
Whilst southerly the path leads up, across a grassy meadow.

I stroll along, my heart at ease, whilst 'Spider' dog explores around,
Decoding woodland gossip from smells intense on plant and ground.

E'en though the path we're treading is one trodden week on week
Each walk is an adventure, as nature's clues we seek.

Here a deer has stopped to browse, scraping ground for mossy treat,
And there's a badger's nightly trail, clearly mapped by scuffling feet.

All about is evidence plain, of military endeavour; bullets spent -
Foxholes once used - and levelled site (where once pitched tent).

Within the trees we hear birds call, and sometimes glimpse a flash of feather
Whilst above, the rooks soar high, hard-pressed to fly in windy weather.

And all around, this springtime morn, yellow catkins tails are swinging,
The primrose, earthbound, brightly blooms 'neath beech trees sticky budding.

Now we have reached the lakeside dell, the limit of our path
Where we will turn back homewards; but first my dog must bath.

He eases down the steep shoreline to nose at water's edge
Then paddles in, to swim about (alarming ducks from nests of eggs).

When he emerges, dripping wet, his temperament has changed,
He scurries round, and barks a lot, and acts as though deranged.

On our way home one last adventure, when we meet a friendly dog
With whom to leap and chase around and wrestle over fallen log.

And now our day's walk's ended, for me, my dog and I.
But tomorrow we'll stroll out again, what, pray, will we espy?

Gary Pike

GARDEN BIRDS

I wish I were a bird,
They don't need clothes or money,
They fly away each autumn
To where it's warm and sunny,
And those who spend the winter here
Are fed on nuts and fat and crumbs,
Then perch on trees above my car
To empty all their bums.
When next door's cat comes hunting
They fly away in fear,
Then sit upon the chimney pots
Chirping insults with a sneer.
They push their young out of the nest
As soon as they can flutter,
Thus never suffer teenage birds
Who fill the house with clutter.
No wonder birds can sing all day
And flit from tree to tree,
The songs I hear them carol, say -
  'I bet you wish to be
    A garden bird, a happy bird,
      A little bird like me!'

Pauline M Parlour

THE MISSING RAVENS

Where have the two young ravens gone?
With beaks shaded clerical grey,
And eyes diamond-bright as anthracite coal,
Just to where did those birds fly away?

Where have the two young ravens gone?
Which sat on the posts for crumbs
In their business-like plumage they've moved elsewhere.
Will they return when the winter comes?

Where have the two young ravens gone?
With croaking cries like frogs with colds
Leaving their trees in summer's moist air
Plus their favourite branches toeholds?

Where have the two young ravens gone?
In their habits of funeral black,
Swooping and diving like bats at eve,
Will they ever come back?

Where have the two young ravens gone?
Resident squirrels held them at bay,
Facing them like knights of old.
Maybe, that's why they did not stay?

Where have the two young ravens gone?
Are they wandering far and wide?
Yet, all being well, they'll remember the way,
And return to their own countryside.

Loré Föst

DEFINE A CANINE

I love my dog, my four-legged companion loves me,
Together we make good company.
He enjoys a nice cuddle, massage and comb of a coat shiny and lush,
His tail is impressive, resembles the one sported by Basil Brush . . .

He is more than a dog, he's an individual, a friend,
He's an intelligent being on whom I can depend.
He knows kindness, loyalty, patience and trust,
He's a guardian, part of the family, for me he's a must.

You can't hide his leader, he hears the sound straight away,
His body clock and rhythm inform him of the time of day.
That big rudder starts swishing, there is a bright light in his eye,
If you look sternly at him, say, 'Not yet,' he immediately
                                      questions, 'Why?'

When out on our walks, I like to watch him run free,
To enjoy the sights, sounds and scents of the lovely country.
He paddles in the sea, races up hills, delights in woodland trails,
Our bond has been forged in all seasons, sunshine, blizzards and gales.

With good nosh inside him and a bite on his bone,
He settles in his favourite spot by the fire with a contented moan.
Paws at full stretch, choice place on the mat,
Only one thing would move him, have you guessed right? A cat.

My pal is alert in the house, protects his domain,
Over the garden and building maintains supreme reign.
No trespasser or stranger would make any advance,
He would respond and take a firm grip in any circumstance.

His needs are simple, his nature unspoiled
He doesn't require the things for which I have toiled.
His world is full of wonder, like that of a child,
Yes, I believe I can learn from him, and the 'call of the wild'.

Dennis Overton

MOON

When I see the moon, shining high up in the sky,
It seems to smile at me, as I walk on by,
It guides me, on my way, in the dark of night.

I love to see the moon shine, on a cold, dark, clear night,
When the full moon is shining, it is a pleasant sight,
As it guides me, on my way,
On this dark, cold, winter night.

The moon is so clear and bright,
As it guides me, on my way, as I walk by,
On this cold, dark, winter night.

Trevor Howarth

MY HAMSTER KEVIN

My hamster Kevin is not very big
But very small
I enjoy watching him run around in
His hamster ball.

In his cage at night he chews the bars
Keeps me up all night awake
I've shouted at him once
'Kevin, for goodness sake!'

Looking at his little brown face
He doesn't care
People say he looks like a teddy bear
With his light brown face
Dimples around his nose
Big, pink, soft toes.

He loves to eat everything
Cucumber is his best
He stuffs it in his pouch
And hides it with the rest.

He is so very friendly
He listens to my voice
He runs onto my bed to be honest
I have no choice

Now he's started to get tired
He's now a geriatric who's retired
He's slow in his ball
He has to stop and rest
Gets a little short of breath.

He sleeps a lot more
Looks a little grey
It's drawing close to that sad, unhappy day
I am hoping he will go to sleep and not wake
Or I am in a dream and it's all a mistake.

My cage is to stand empty
Clean and bare
Poor Kevin, my brown teddy bear.

My cage is to stand empty
No hamster to be seen
Just memories of what had been.

Carly Rosewell

THE GARDEN

I'm sat in the garden, what a lovely sight,
Roses, Marigolds and Daisies, all bright,
How pleasant to sit here when all work is done
It's been lots of hard work and I guess, some fun.
There are silent birds on the wing fluttering around,
Blackbird, Thrush, and Blue Tits abound.
All this makes a very colourful scene
It also relaxes and calms, do you know what I mean?
I've just seen a patch that could do with turning over,
And the grass over their needs a turn with the mower.
But after all work is done
I sit here with a cup of tea and a bun!
Such a calming effect a garden has,
Amid all the flowers, the birds and green grass.
So take some time off and pull up a chair -
And let us together - a garden share.

Joyce M Robinson

GUS

Tim had an owl - its name was Gus
It really was a sight
It kept its head beneath its wings
While flying through the night.

It wished it was a different bird
A Sparrow, Tit or Lark
Because, poor Gus, it's sad to say
Was frightened of the dark.

Tim did not know quite what to do
To try to help his bird
Whatever tricks he thought about
Were really quite absurd.

A dynamo, with bulb in front
To show his Gus the way
A candle on a helmet
Might turn night into day.

A friendly flock of fireflies
Or glow-worms in his beak
- That could be quite expensive,
He'd eat hundreds in a week!

And then Tim said to Gus, 'Don't fret,
Don't worry - it's all right!
If you don't like the dark - okay!
Just wait until it's light!'

Nicolette A Bodilly

BEAUTY

Beauty is all around us, when we look,
The wayside trees, and flowers, the pebble brook.
Lush meadows, where a horse runs free,
Red-painted ladybirds - brown humming bee.
A sulphur butterfly's translucent wings,
A Blackbird in the orchard where he sings
Grey sheep, and woolly lambs within the fold -
Frost on the hedgerows when the days are cold,
And spider's webs, all glistening with dew.
Bluebells on hedge banks, but to name a few.
The morning sunrise, and a rainbow bright
A radiant sunset's all suffusing light.
A wily fox who enters on the scene,
His red coat and white front so clearly seen
And rabbits with white tails a-bobbing round,
Where luminous green glow-worms may be found.
The silver stars which twinkle up above
A tawny night-owl, and a cooing dove.
The lamp which from a cottage doorway shines
On pink-hued roses, clematis and vines.
Night-scented stocks, pink, purple, cream and white
Pervading perfume through the stilly night.
And variegated ivy on the wall
Protecting robin's young from sudden squall.
The tiny wren, a chaffinch and a thrush
Singing in chorus from the holly bush.
A jay which spreads it's pink and blue-black wings
And to the praise of God and nature sings.
Beauty before our eyes if - 'Full of care
We still can stand, and find the time to stare.'

Kathleen Cork

Sunflower

S earching for the warmth of the summer sun, to radiate your seasonal beauty,
U nusually tall, you are the gentle giant of the flowering domain.
N ature's curious creatures scamper upon numerous silken petals,
F ree to leisurely gaze upon the glorious garden below.
L ike the shy butterfly, you conceal your brilliance until it's time,
O nly then do you display your combination of colour and fascination.
W ater trickles sleepily across your darkened seeds, to replenish the soft green grass beneath you.
E mbrace the sweltering heat, which feeds your blazing appetite for existence.
R each up with enduring pride, my magnificent companion!

Sue Pearce

TRANSIENCE

The sea is calm.
    The wind is fair,
        Sweet is the air!

The golden sun shimmers upon the silver sea.

The waves are ruffled.
    The wind blows past,
        The sky is overcast.

The tide is rising.
    The wind whistles by,
        Dark is the sky.

The ocean is rough.
    The wind roars loudly,
        The sky's black and cloudy.

The breakers are billowing,
    The wind is screaming
        The rain is teeming.

The thunder is raging,
    The fierce gale lashes
        The lighting flashes!

The storm recedes.
    The squall has ceased.
        I am at peace.

The golden sun gleams upon the silver sea.

Christine Lemon

CHANGING SCENES

There's so much to enjoy every day
As we wonder on life's way
The changing scenes down a quiet lane
As it weaves by fields of shades of green
Round each bend there's something new
Just waiting there for you
To gladden your heart and give you joy
Such wonders spring from nature's Earth
The little flowers, their faces to the sun
Look so fragile yet they are so strong
To push their way through rich, brown earth
Yet each year they give new birth
The hedgerows in coats of emerald green
Also add to that wonderful scene
A wild rose clings there looks pale and weak
Yet it adds such a gentle streak
The dewy pearls left on the grass
From the shower that's just pasted
And there in the eye of that upturned flower
A raindrop sparkles just like a tear
The breeze warm and gentle drifts slowly by
And feathery clouds drift way up high
The patterns and pictures on every side
Stretch out there far and wide
I would like to take it all to frame
For next time I pass this way
The changing scenes will have changed again.

Joan Wright

A Sting In The Tail

To be a bee, or not to be - that is the question.

But what would the world do without me?
You don't seem to like me, but I'm the one with the power
To transfer the pollen from flower to flower.
A 'must' for all fruits - and vegetables too.
What would our world do if nothing grew?

I need a safe place for building my hive
Where I can make honey, to keep grubs alive.
But if I settle near Man, and gather my throng
He smokes me out, and moves me along.
What a pity it is people don't see a thing
Except my sweet honey . . .

And how hard I sting.

Helen Walker

STROLLING

I went for a stroll, the other day,
To Cherry Hinton Hall, I made my way,
Watching different birds in flight,
And scampering squirrels, a cheerful sight.

Mother's, with youngsters, on the swings,
Others, playing with various things.
Then off to the lake, to enjoy the view,
Many others, had gone there too.

Lots of ducks and swans, were there,
Swimming around to get their share,
Of all the scraps of food thrown in,
And children seeing which one would win.

It's a walk I like to do,
To meander around, for a mile or two.
Then it's 'homeward bound' for a cup of tea,
And a fulfilling 'stroll' was had by me.

It is said, 'The best things in life are free!'
So! Enjoy the pleasures, that you can see,
Remember! A cheerful word, and a friendly smile,
All helps to make life, well worthwhile.

Eddie Lawrence

AN EVENING WALK

Isn't it great to find a path
that goes you know not where?
You veer to the left and head for a lake
to see whatever is there.

A heron standing tall and still,
two swans with their little brood.
You continue round and find a path
meandering through a wood.

Out in the open the path goes on
through the waving tall green grass,
an iridescent dragonfly,
hovering as you pass.

You climb a hill, and at the top
look out across the view,
spreading out before you
fragrant, green and new.

Too far to go, you must turn back,
but larks fly high above,
they can't be seen but sing their song
so joyously in love.

Your heart is filled with thankfulness
that you chose to come this way,
for the peace and calm you found here,
aborts a stressful day.

Pat Hayward

THE ROSE

Take from me my love, my valentine
this rose of ruby red
care for it and water it
lest it will die and bow its head

Reminds me in its beauty and grace
of you my only sweetheart
I'm sending it with all my love
bare your soul and say we will never part

Cupid leaps from cloud to cloud
arrows of loveliness he shoots
he drew upon this one lovely rose
and spliced it from it's roots

A shroud of sheer perfection
in emerald green and red I see
the only other beauty I behold
is when I dream of thee

Look upon its beauty and grace
so elegant and so slender
and every time you see this rose
think of me its sender.

Catherine Watson

MOTHER NATURE

Sitting down to view a scene
Where Mother Nature reigns supreme,
The jigsaw puzzle always finished,
No valley misplaced or hillside diminished

Birds soar on her glove-puppeted hand,
And dance in the face of her heart flaming brand

Mother Nature shines this eve
On her work of stone, grass, tree and leaf

Her puzzle never left undone,
The sun, the moon, the Earth, her son.

Mark Wood

I Spider

Threads of silver carefully woven
Sunlight dancing
Bright and golden

Morning dew like tear from eye
Spider awaits unsuspecting fly

Tied invisibly, tied to the air
Workmanship beyond compare

Tightrope walker, master of trapeze
Gently swaying on the breeze

Out of sight your eight arms feel
Awaiting arrival of mid-day meal

Maureen Gilbert

A Dewdrop On A Rose

Most gracious, heavenly, royal rose,
Oh may I capture, fondle and behold
The beauty that within your crimson folds
You clasp. A teeny dewdrop in repose
Pure as the child which Mary's arms enclose.
From mists of morn conceived, a birth untold,
Cradled by love in softest satin, behold
This princely pearl from diadems unfroze.

Upon your face you show the grace of God,
Your breath flows from His firmament on High'
When welcome winds caress, you gently nod
And shed your charm to travellers passing by.
What wealth doth lie beneath this sod,
Yet mortal men still starve the roots of good.

M Newble

A PONY TALE

I wonder what the ponies think, as they stand at the gate,
And watch me at the window, as I wash and wipe the plates.
Are they thinking it is dinner time, or have we just had tea?
I wonder what they're thinking, as they watch busy me.

I think they are so fortunate out in the fields all day.
Lots of lovely things to see, nature's fine display.
Birds up in the treetops, building nests so merrily.
Squirrels in the hedgerows collecting nuts for tea.

Fox cubs playing in the grass having lots of fun.
And the baby rabbits out of the burrows run.
All of nature's wonderland, they have time to see
Cos ponies are not busy, unlike you or me.

Jean Ledwards

How Can I Work?

How can I work with a great big nose,
Cold and shiny, pushing under my arm?
It's inspiration I suppose,
And part of his hairy charm.

This great big nose is wet and grubby,
With jowls all slimy and damp.
Why can't you go and pester hubby?
You're depriving me of writer's cramp.

His great big paws pad to the next room,
Ah, peace at last it seems.
Then I hear the product all too soon,
It seems peace is in my dreams.

For the next I hear is splosh, gulp, slurp.
He drinks from the toilet pan!
He finishes it off, with a resonant burp,
Then he's back where he first began!

Angela White

A DOG'S LIFE - THROUGH PETRA'S EYES
(Written for my dog Petra, 1990)

I nuzzle her, I kiss her face
I look at her, I leave no trace
I wish she'd wake, I want her to
No one loves her like I do
The seconds pass, minutes fly
Oh please wake up, I want to cry
Another kiss, she turns her cheek
She gently moans, she has a peek
She reaches out and touches me
Her eyes are shut, they do not see
She stretches, puts out her leg
I watch her as I sit and beg
She pats me says good day to me
And I'm as happy as can be,
I wag my tail, I'm pleased to say
This is the way I start each day

Ann Nelson

SKYLARK

Oh little bird
Up in the sky
How do you fly
So very high?

I flap my wings
And up I go
Just how that works
I do not know

But work it does
As my wings beat
I see the Earth
Below retreat

I glide around
Without a care
Catching some flies
Here and there

And as I soar
Around I sing
And manoeuvre about
With the dip of a wing

I nest on the ground
And fly sun up till dark
What sort of bird am I?
Why, I'm a skylark

D W Mynott

TAFF MY FRIEND

A friend is one who's always there
To sit and tell your troubles to
He sits and looks and tries to understand
Then comes along and licks my hand
And in his way tries to say
'Please don't be sad'
He brings his ball, come let's play
Forget your troubles for today
I'll be with you when you need a friend
Be by your side come what may
I'll be with you forever and a day
If thinking who can this person be
It's my dog 'Taff' and he's very true to me

B Green

CATS

Cats are superior animals
They walk with unimaginable pride
Sure, they're cute and cuddly
Hang on a minute, I think I lied

They claw at the carpet
And bring you small gifts
Be it a mouse, a bird, a huge moth or two
I wouldn't be without them
They have good qualities too

They're clean if you're lucky
They're good listeners too
They enjoy a good fuss
And the love they return
But that could be because we feed them
Will we ever learn?

Gemma Doughty

The Yearly Clipping In June Of Seymour Butts, A Fine But Fat Half Lakeland Terrier

He hides; always he hides, behind the table or settee.
Has he not learned, the senseless dog, he never will escape from me?
I pull him from his dusty haunt, his silence and his distant stare
Tell everything to me! I know that he would rather not be there!

And now what, now that he's been caught? If I do not remain alert
Whilst plugging in the clippers, he'll jump off the table, risking hurt.
There's three stones of him, four small legs, yet he is not afraid to try it
Despite a visit to the vet last week who told him he *must* diet.

Upon the kitchen table sits my sad and tubby little boy.
The other dogs lie just beneath, the more his anguish to enjoy.
I trim his furry ginger legs and when I ask him just to stand
He'll look at me with languid eyes then sit down hard upon my hand!

His bottom he would rather do himself, of that I am quite sure,
But as he cannot reach it then in me his trust he's forced to store.
I'm very careful as I trim around those parts that dogs hold dear
And notice how he flinches if he thinks I may have gone too near!

His face is next. The clippers stop. My little scissors take him now
And gently, softly, trim his ears, his chin, his eyes, his nose, his brow.
How smart he looks, I proudly think. I turn away to reach a comb.
He's off the table like a flash and that is why I wrote this poem!

I wanted everyone to know that portly Seymour Butts and I
Are usually on such good terms except in June when fur must fly.
My dog will not co-operate. Why does he squirm and fidget
When afterwards he's sleek and cool and I know he's glad I did it?

Lesley S Robinson

ANCHOR BOOKS SUBMISSIONS INVITED
SOMETHING FOR EVERYONE

ANCHOR BOOKS - Any subject, light-hearted clean fun, nothing unprintable please.

THE OPPOSITE SEX - Have your say on the opposite gender. Do they drive you mad or can we co-exist in harmony?

THE NATURAL WORLD - Are we destroying the world around us? What should we do to preserve the beauty and the future of our planet - you decide!

All poems no longer than 30 lines.
Always welcome! No fee!
Plus cash prizes to be won!

Mark your envelope (eg *The Natural World*)
And send to:
Anchor Books
Remus House, Coltsfoot Drive
Peterborough, PE2 9JX

OVER £10,000 IN POETRY PRIZES TO BE WON!

Send an SAE for details on our New Year 2003 competition!